Acknowledgments

To the chroniclers of the outlaw West.

John Muir Publications, P.O. Box 613, Santa Fe, New Mexico 87504
© 1994 by John Muir Publications
All rights reserved. Published 1994
Printed in the United States of America

First edition. First printing August 1994
          First TWG printing August 1994

Library of Congress Cataloging-in-Publication Data
Gintzler, A. S.
Rough and ready outlaws and lawmen / A. S. Gintzler
  p.   cm.
Includes index.
ISBN 1-56261-163-1 : $12.95
1. Outlaws—West (U.S.)—History—19th century—Juvenile literature. 2. Peace officers—
West (U.S.)—History—19th century—Juvenile literature. 3. Frontier and pioneer life—West
(U.S.)—History—19th century—Juvenile literature. 4. West (U.S.)—History—19th cen-
tury—Juvenile literature. [1. Robbers and outlaws—West (U.S.) 2. Peace officers—West
(U.S.) 3. Frontier and pioneer life—West (U.S.) 4. West (U.S.)—History.] I. Title.
F596.G575 1994
978'.02—dc20   94-4039
                                      CIP
                                      AC

Logo Design: Chris Brigman
Interior Design and Typography: Linda Braun
Illustrations: Chris Brigman
Printer: Arcata Graphics/Kingsport

Distributed to the book trade by
W. W. Norton & Co., Inc.
500 Fifth Avenue
New York, NY 10110

Distributed to the education market by
The Wright Group
19201 120th Avenue N.E.
Bothell, WA 98011-9512

Cover photo, Dodge City Peace Commission, 1882, The Bettmann Archive
Back cover photo, Jesse James in 1864, age 17, The Bettmann Archive
Title page photo, Company D Texas Rangers, 1894, Western History Collections, University
   of Oklahoma Library

Western History Collections, University of Oklahoma Library

*The Modoc stagecoach in
Tombstone, Arizona*

CONTENTS

THE WILD WEST

THE OUTLAWS

THE LAWMEN

Law and Disorder in the West

The frontier West of the 1800s was a wild and mostly lawless land until lawmen and legal courts arrived. Pioneers from the eastern states had moved west for land and riches. It was a while before law officers, courts, and jails caught up to the rush of western settlers. Outlaws were a lot quicker.

Explorers, trappers, and traders blazed the first trails through the western wilderness. Land-hungry farmers and gold-hungry prospectors followed the new trails, while gamblers, thieves, and outlaws also rushed west, one step ahead of the law.

Most western settlers were honest people. They brought with them a culture that valued freedom and hard work. But some pioneers who came west didn't respect the law. They thought that violence and dishonesty were the best ways to get ahead.

Violence had been a part of American life since colonial times. In Boston, colonists had rioted against English rule. Supporters of England were tortured and killed in the streets. Riots continued even after America won independence from England. Slavery in the South also bred violence. And white settlers had been fighting Indians right from the start.

Colonists protesting British rule rioted in Boston

GUNFIGHTERS AND GUNMEN

Throughout the West, professional gunfighters, called "gunmen," made a living from their shooting skills. Honest lawmen like Bass Reeves used guns only when they had to. But lawmen like Wild Bill Hickok were gunmen first and lawmen second. Wild Bill killed even when he didn't have to. Outlaws like Wes Hardin were also professional gunmen, but on the wrong side of the law. There were also "hired guns" like Jim Miller who would kill a man if someone paid him to do it.

A Colt six-shooter

The Bettmann Archive

Between 1834 and 1860, there were 35 riots in U.S. cities. Mobs attacked Catholics in Pennsylvania, Mormons in Missouri, and Germans in Kentucky. Mob violence moved west with pioneer farmers, miners, and railroaders. Settlers on the Kansas-Missouri border began fighting over slavery in the 1850s. The outlaw Jesse James and the lawman Wild Bill Hickok fought on different sides in the border wars.

Gunmen often rode along with wagon trains of settlers heading west across the Plains

In 1861, American violence finally exploded into civil war. Thousands of working men signed up as soldiers, ready to kill or die for their cause. By the time the war ended, many more hearts were hardened to death and violence. Feelings of distrust and hatred between North and South didn't end with the war. In 1865, many Civil War veterans headed for the western frontier—and they didn't hang up their guns.

In the first three years after the Civil War, there were more than a thousand killings in Texas. Former slaves were beaten, tortured, and hanged by angry citizens who had fought for the South and lost. There were few lawmen to stop them. Mobs of gunmen rode wild on the Texas plains, while the James-Younger gang robbed trains and banks in Missouri.

On the cattle and mining frontiers, honest citizens began taking the law into their own hands. They couldn't wait for lawmen, courts, and judges to bring law and order to their towns.

While the culture of violence began in the East, it exploded in the West. Wide open spaces, cattle and horses, gold and silver, and six-guns bred the gunfighter. Outlaws robbed trains, banks, and stagecoaches. The old West wasn't always violent, though. Cowtowns like Abilene, Kansas, and mining towns like Tombstone, Arizona, didn't have killings every night. They had fewer than two murders per year. But there were exceptions. In 1881, five men were killed in Tombstone—three of them by lawmen.

Western pioneers sometimes settled disputes with their fists

Vigilantes and Lynch Law

As honest settlers pushed west for land and gold, so did law-breakers and fugitives from justice. On the frontier, outlaws found even more room for dishonest work. There were few lawmen and legal courts to stop them, so groups of citizens called vigilantes took the law into their own hands.

One of the first vigilante groups was formed in Virginia while the American colonies were still a part of England. In 1780, a Virginia settler named Charles Lynch organized a vigilante group to stop horse thieves. These vigilantes were like a citizens' police force. They caught criminals and brought them to trial. Since there weren't any real courts yet, trials were held in unofficial "people's courts."

Lynch and other settlers acted as judges to decide innocence or guilt. Men found guilty of horse stealing were hung by their thumbs, whipped, then run out of town. This vigilante system of justice became known as "lynch law." It spread with the frontier into the western territories.

Vigilante groups formed in California's gold fields during the 1850s. Honest prospectors banded together to stop theft and violence in mining camps and towns. In 1849, the citizens of San Francisco formed a vigilante group to stop an outlaw gang called the Hounds. Some 400 vigilantes rounded up the outlaws, tried them in a people's court, and kicked them out of town. But San Francisco's trouble with outlaws was just beginning.

Posters like this one warned criminals to get out of town or risk being lynched

HANGTOWN, CALIFORNIA

In 1849, a gang of thieves was caught in the California mining town called Dry Diggings. Since the town had no legal courts, local miners formed a people's court and held a trial. The thieves were found guilty and punished by whipping. Three of the gang members were then accused of other crimes and found guilty again. The miners voted to hang them and wasted no time doing it. From then until 1851, the town was called "Hangtown."

Criminals from as far away as Australia were among the thousands who joined the California Gold Rush in 1849. San Francisco's law officers just couldn't keep up with all the theft and murder caused by outlaw gangs. In 1851, citizens formed a "vigilance committee" to bring law and order to San Francisco. They captured, judged, and hanged two Australian criminals, then went after others.

California state officials objected to the hangings, but the citizens of San Francisco didn't. By 1856, the vigilance committee had 8,000 members. Outlaws fled San Francisco, fearing the vigilantes and lynch law.

Vigilante groups also formed on the cattle frontier to deal with cattle rustlers, horse thieves, and murderers. Horse stealing was thought to be as evil as murder, since survival on the range depended on having a horse. Ranchers, cowboys, and townspeople banded together to stop outlaw gangs. But vigilantes in cattle country often didn't bother with trials.

Vigilante groups booted outlaws out of town

In 1876, the citizens of Fort Griffin, Texas, formed a secret vigilante group. Under cover of night, they captured and hanged cattle and horse thieves. In June 1876, the vigilantes pulled two horse thieves from the Albany, Texas, jail and hanged them without a trial. Such hangings came to be called lynchings, and lynch law took on a new, ugly meaning.

Vigilante groups were a first step in bringing law and order to the western frontier. But in some ways, vigilantes made the frontier even more lawless because they lynched people without fair trials. Some vigilante groups were more like angry lynch mobs than honest citizens' police and courts.

Angry citizens took John Heith from an Arizona jail and lynched him on a telephone pole

Frontier Feuds

Texas cattle country was a hotbed of lawlessness and violence in the West. Criminals from the eastern states fled there to escape the reach of law. There were few courts or lawmen on the cattle frontier, but plenty of guns. Ranchers, cowboys, and cattle thieves settled disputes with their own bullets.

The Larned City, Kansas, prison in 1886

One killing often led to another and snowballed into feuds or local civil wars. Neighbors, families, and friends chose sides to get revenge. Sometimes entire communities got caught up in the violence—as they did in Shelby County, Texas, in 1840.

A Shelby County man named Charles Jackson killed his neighbor Joseph Goodbread after an argument. Jackson was charged with murder and jailed. But a dishonest sheriff let him go free to await trial. Instead of hiring a lawyer, Jackson got ready for his trial by threatening and killing Goodbread's friends.

Jackson formed a gang called the Regulators that pretended to go after horse thieves, but really went after Jackson's enemies. At Jackson's trial, the Regulators, armed with guns, filled the courtroom. The judge fled in fear and the frightened jury found Jackson innocent. Angry citizens and Goodbread's friends then formed their own gang, called the Moderators.

Regulators and Moderators feuded, or battled, on the east Texas plains for three years. Gang members were ambushed on lonely roads, burned out of their homes, or lynched. Peaceful settlers were forced at gunpoint to take sides. When the district court judge tried to investigate local murders, Regulators pointed a cannon at the courthouse.

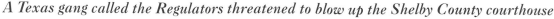

A Texas gang called the Regulators threatened to blow up the Shelby County courthouse

In 1844, Regulators posted a list of names on the courthouse door. The list included Moderators, local citizens, and public officials who were warned to leave town, or else. About 165 Moderators then rode out to fight the Regulators and their leader, Watt Moorman. The feuding didn't stop until the Texas militia invaded Shelby County and arrested gang leaders.

The longest and bloodiest frontier feud began in Dewitt County, Texas, in 1866. It began when rancher Charles Taylor was accused of horse stealing. Bill Sutton organized a group of armed citizens, called a posse, that rode out and killed Taylor. A few months later, Buck Taylor, Charles' relative, tried to get revenge on Sutton, but he too was killed. The Sutton-Taylor feud had begun.

Kin—family members—on both sides went gunning for each other. Soon, two more Taylor men were killed and Bill Sutton was wounded. Years passed. In 1870, two Taylor friends were kidnapped by Suttons and shot dead in an open field.

Feuding continued into 1873, when two Sutton men were ambushed by Taylors. Soon after, three Taylors were lynched by Suttons. By this time, Bill Sutton had married and grown tired of the feud. He decided to leave Texas, but couldn't escape the violence he'd started. As he and his wife boarded a ship for New Orleans, two Taylor men gunned him down.

Sutton's death did not end the feud. Suttons and Taylors continued to kill and be killed until 1881, when Texas Rangers brought the Suttons to trial.

THE TEXAS RANGERS

In 1823, when Texas was still part of Mexico, Comanches and other Indians raided Texas settlers. To stop these attacks, Mexico's governor hired a force of 15 men. These were the first Texas Rangers. When Texas fought Mexico for independence 12 years later, 150 Texas Rangers joined the struggle. Texas became a state in 1845, and the Rangers were made a statewide law enforcement agency. However, in modern times, the Texas Rangers have been accused of mistreating Mexican Americans in Texas. The old Texas Ranger style of frontier justice is often unequal and unfair.

The Frontier Battalion of the Texas Rangers in 1894

Western History Collections, University of Oklahoma Library

The Range Wars

Frontier violence exploded into all-out wars on the cattle ranges of the West. Cattlemen, farmers, sheepherders, and hired gunmen fought bloody "range wars" over land and water. Out on the frontier, far from any courtroom, men took justice into their own hands. Outlaws like Billy the Kid and Butch Cassidy began their careers during this time.

The wars were caused by fierce competition on the cattle range of the Great Plains. The first Texas cattlemen started their herds from wild and stray cattle. Many of these cows had been stolen, or "rustled," from Mexican cattlemen. Cowboys were hired to steal cows, brand them, and drive them to market. There were no laws against this, and no lawmen to stop them. On the unfenced open range, the only mark of ownership was the brand burned into a cow's flesh.

Ranchers fighting over an unbranded cow

Many honest cowboys started their own herds this way. It was perfectly legal—only because there weren't any laws yet. But dishonest cowboys like Butch Cassidy went a step further and became professional cattle thieves. They raided other men's herds, changed the brands, and sold the cows.

By the 1880s, there were few stray cows left. With the invention of barbed wire, wealthy cattlemen began fencing their lands to keep cattle thieves out. Some of this land they owned. But they also fenced public lands and water supplies. In Texas, cattlemen and farmers who had been fenced out of grazing lands and water holes cut through fences to get to the grass and water.

A Western sheep farm

On the plains of Wyoming, wealthy cattlemen accused homesteaders and small-time ranchers of cattle stealing. In 1889, they lynched a homesteader named James Averill, then went after other suspected rustlers. Small ranchers fought back in the Johnson County War. In 1892, the wealthy cattlemen transported a small army of professional gunmen by train from Texas. They battled in Wyoming's Powder River country until the U.S. Army arrived to stop the fighting.

Wealthy ranchers accused the fence cutters of rustling. They formed cattlemen's associations and hired armed guards to protect the fenced range lands. Small ranchers turned to the government for help, but rich cattlemen were above the law. Wealth and power enabled them to buy off law enforcers. Fence cutting continued in the dark of night. Farmers and small ranchers banded together in groups with names like the Javelines, Owls, and Blue Devils. They took down fences and battled the hired gunmen.

Range wars followed barbed wire fences north from Texas and across cattle country. In Nebraska, farmers cut fences and built homes on public lands that cattlemen had fenced off. More violence broke out when homesteaders brought sheep into cattle country.

Wealthy cattlemen tried to force sheepherders off the range. They hired gunmen to slaughter entire flocks. In Garfield County, Colorado, gunmen stampeded 3,800 sheep off a bluff into Parachute Creek below. Flocks were dynamited, poisoned, and clubbed to death while sheepherders were killed in their sleep.

In Johnson County, Wyoming, sheepherders fought back. They joined small-time cattlemen and homesteaders in their struggle against the wealthy ranchers. Fighting over land and water led to the Johnson County War in 1892.

Professional cattle thieves took advantage of the disorder and lawlessness. While fence cutters battled the cattlemen's armies, rustlers made off with the cows. In Lincoln County, New Mexico, sheepherders and small ranch owners clashed with powerful cattlemen. Hired killers were in great demand. Small armies of cowboys and gunmen like Billy the Kid fought the bloody Lincoln County War—a war without winners.

Cattle ranchers dynamited flocks of sheep to force sheepherders off the range

Boom Towns

wns on the western frontier "boomed" practically overnight. After gold was discovered in California in 1848, thousands of gold seekers rushed west. San Francisco grew from a town of less than a thousand to a city of 25,000 in just one year. Boom towns also followed the railroad west and were the end of the line for cattle on the great trail drives.

Mining towns, railroad towns, and cattle towns became centers for trade and business on the western frontier.

Prospectors, railroad workers, homesteaders, and traders passed through or settled in these frontier towns. So did swindlers, gamblers, and outlaws looking for easy money.

Cripple Creek, Colorado, was a Western boom town

Some outlaws headed for mining towns like Tombstone, Arizona, and Deadwood, South Dakota, where they tried to steal gold and silver shipments coming out of the mines. Cowtowns like Abilene, Wichita, and Dodge City, Kansas, attracted cattle rustlers and horse thieves.

In these early boom towns, disorder ruled. In mining towns, dishonest prospectors "jumped claims," stealing other miners' gold. Miners had to write their own codes of law and police themselves. They had no jails, courts, or lawmen. Theft, violence, and murder in the gold fields had to be dealt with swiftly.

"Popular juries" composed of local miners decided a man's innocence or guilt—usually guilt. Punishment was by whipping, hanging, maiming, or branding. In one mining camp, a miner named George Gillin received 39 lashes for stealing another man's gold.

Even saloons were used as courtrooms in some towns

The mining town of Leadville, Colorado

In time, law officers and legal courts caught up with the frontier towns. By the 1870s, county sheriffs, town marshals, and U.S. marshals were policing the western frontier. But in a region used to lawlessness, citizens often continued to take the law into their own hands.

In Abilene, Kansas, railroad tracks divided the town right down the middle. On one side lived Abilene's law-abiding citizens. On the other side were stockyards, saloons, and gambling halls. This was "Texas Abilene," named for the cowboys who cut loose there after driving cattle up the trails from Texas. A jail and courthouse were under construction in 1870 when "Bear River" Tom Smith became Abilene's first town marshal. Smith enforced a town law against carrying guns, until he was killed by a murder suspect.

Sharpshooter Wild Bill Hickok followed Smith as marshal and also enforced the town ban on guns. Cowboys were ordered to leave their six-shooters at the horse stable or with bartenders. The laws banning firearms kept cowboys and gamblers from settling arguments with bullets. But Hickok himself was run out of Abilene after killing two men with his Colt pistol.

Deadwood, South Dakota, had a gambling and saloon district called the "Badlands." In 1876, outlaws Sam Bass and Joel Collins formed a gang there with "Gentleman Jack" Davis to rob stagecoaches. Tombstone, Arizona, was also considered an outlaw town. There were five killings there in 1881—but three of them were by lawmen, the Earps and Doc Holliday.

DODGE CITY, KANSAS

Legend says 15 to 25 men were killed in Dodge City and "died with their boots on" in 1872. They were buried in a poor man's graveyard called Boot Hill. Lawlessness ruled Dodge through much of its history. Town officials owned saloons and made money from cowboys' drinking and gambling. Lawmen like Bat Masterson and his brothers weren't always successful at enforcing gun laws. Ed Masterson was killed in 1878 while trying to disarm a drunken cowboy. There were five killings that year in Dodge.

Boot Hill was the end of the trail for many cowboys

Stagecoach Holdups

Before railroads covered the West, horse-drawn or mule-drawn stage-coaches carried travelers, payrolls, and gold and silver from western mines. Outlaws called "road agents" or "highwaymen" stopped and robbed these stages on deserted roads. They hid at the top of steep hills where tired horse and mule teams slowed to a walk. Then they jumped out from behind trees and bushes with pistols and Winchester rifles.

It usually took three men to rob a stage. One held the horses' reins while another pointed a gun at the driver and passengers. The third raided the strongbox, or safe, that held gold, silver, or cash. But some road agents chose to work alone. Charles E. Boles, better known as "Black Bart," single-handedly held up 28 Wells Fargo stages in California.

Black Bart robbed his first Wells Fargo stage on July 26, 1875. He jumped out of hiding waving a double-barreled shotgun and ordered the driver to throw down the strongbox. In 1877, after holding up a stage near Duncan's Mills, Black Bart left behind a poem. Newspaper reporters soon began calling him the "bandit poet."

Black Bart continued to rob stages all along the California coast. Then in 1883, he acci-dentally drop-ped a silk handkerchief at the scene of a holdup. Detectives traced a laundry mark on the cloth to a San Fran-cisco shop and found out the customer's name. Black Bart served five years in prison for armed robbery.

Black Bart was known as the "bandit poet"

Nevada's Milton Sharp had an even longer career as a stage robber. Around 1869, Sharp began working as a miner near the town of Aurora in Nevada's silver country. He quickly took to rob-bing the stages that carried cash and silver to banks in Carson City. After the robberies, Sharp buried most of his loot in secret locations.

To stop holdups, stage companies hired armed

A Wells Fargo reward poster

The Modoc stagecoach in Tombstone, Arizona

guards to sit next to stagecoach drivers. Since they carried shotguns, these guards were said to be "riding shotgun." Mike Tovey was a Wells Fargo shotgun guard for 28 years. On September 5, 1880, he was guarding a Carson City stage when it was held up by two men. Tovey killed one of them in a gunfight, but the other got away after wounding Tovey in the arm. It was Milton Sharp.

Sharp was trailed to San Francisco, arrested, and found guilty of armed robbery. He escaped from jail, though, by digging a hole through his cell wall. Sharp was caught and returned to prison to serve a 20-year sentence. In August 1889 he escaped a second time and was never heard from again. He may have succeeded in digging up his buried treasure and hiding his identity.

In 1877, the outlaw Sam Bass teamed up with Joel Collins and "Gentleman Jack" Davis to rob stages in the Black Hills gold country of Dakota Territory. They robbed seven stages in a few short months before graduating to train robbery. Bass was killed by Texas Rangers in 1878 after one of his gang betrayed him.

FIRST ARMORED TREASURE COACH

The Cheyenne and Black Hills Stage Company carried gold through the Dakota Territory in the 1870s. The company's Deadwood stage was robbed so many times that it had to stop running. Tighter security was necessary. In 1878, the company ran its first armored "treasure coach" lined with bullet-proof steel plates. It was called the Monitor, after the armored Civil War battleship. But holdup men still found a way to rob it—by shooting through its wooden roof.

Train Robberies

On the night of October 6, 1866, two masked men held up the Ohio & Mississippi Railway in Indiana. The outlaws simply passed through a passenger car and entered the unlocked express car. Express cars carried payroll safes and gold and silver from western mines. Express messengers rode with the precious cargo, but they didn't expect trouble. The masked men surprised the messengers, held them at gunpoint, took $13,000 from the safe, then disappeared into the night. It was the first train robbery in U.S. history.

About a year later, the same train was held up again. A posse rounded up suspects and jailed John Reno. But John had brothers. Four of them held up the Jefferson, Madison, & Indianapolis Railroad, killed a messenger, and got away with $96,000. The Reno Gang entered outlaw history and started a new profession—train robbery. By 1870, the Reno Gang had been captured and lynched. But the age of train robberies was just beginning.

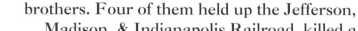

The first western train robbery occurred around midnight on November 5, 1870. A Central Pacific train left Oakland, California, carrying $41,800 in gold coins and $8,800 in silver. In the Wells Fargo Express car, agents were heavily armed with rifles and sawed-off shotguns. As the train slowed down in heavy rain and fog near the town of Verdi, five masked men hopped aboard. Two entered the engine cab with guns pointed at the engineer and fireman. The other three unhooked the express car from the passenger cars.

Robbers held up trains loaded with gold, silver, and cash

While the express car and engine continued up the track, the passenger cars were left behind. Several miles outside of Verdi, the robbers ordered the engineer to stop the train. A sixth outlaw was waiting there with horses. The engine crew was marched back to the express car with guns pointed at their heads. The express agents inside wondered what was going on. They slid open the door and saw five shotguns pointed at them. With no time to reach for their weapons, they surrendered. The outlaws, "Gentleman Jack" Davis and his "Knights of the Road" got away with $41,000 in gold coins.

Pinkerton's National Detective Agency tracked outlaws across the U.S. long before there was an FBI. Railroads hired Pinkerton detectives to bring train robbers to justice. Pinkertons caught the Reno brothers, then went after the James gang and later Butch Cassidy, without success. Around 1900, the Union Pacific Railroad transported detectives on horseback in special train cars to the scene of holdups. Robbers had trouble outrunning these special posses.

The most infamous train robbers of all were Jesse James and his James-Younger gang. They were the first to derail and wreck trains before looting express cars and holding up passengers at gunpoint. Butch Cassidy's Wild Bunch also robbed trains. In the late 1890s, Cassidy formed a secret Train Robber's Syndicate which kept track of gold shipments. They used dynamite to blow open express cars and safes.

In 1890, outlaws robbed a Southern Pacific train of $20,000 in Tulare County, California. The suspects were Chris Evans and John Sontag. They were soon blamed for three more robberies.

The Bettmann Archive

Butch Cassidy's gang kept track of gold shipments so they knew which trains to rob

The Bettmann Archive

When detectives tried to bring them in for questioning, Evans and Sontag killed a deputy and fled. Seven lawmen were wounded in a year-long manhunt through the Sierra mountains. In the end, Sontag was gunned down and Evans was jailed for murder. Evans escaped once, but was returned to prison.

Peaceful train rides were often interrupted by outlaws who robbed passengers at gunpoint

Bank Robberies

Bank robberies were never easy to pull off. Unlike train and stagecoach holdups, bank jobs happened in town, usually in broad daylight. Outlaws who made it to the bank door with bags of cash still had to mount horses and race away without being shot. Even expert bank robbers bungled jobs and went down in a blaze of gunfire.

Two of the Dalton brothers died in 1892 while trying to rob a bank in Coffeyville, Kansas. Three brothers in another outlaw family—Cole, Bob, and Jim Younger—were all wounded and captured after the James-Younger gang robbed a bank in Northfield, Minnesota. Butch Cassidy's Wild Bunch also bungled a bank robbery at Belle Fourche, South Dakota, in 1897.

Bill Doolin rode with the Dalton gang, but survived the Coffeyville bank holdup because he wasn't there. His horse went lame on the way into town and he was left behind. Later, Doolin formed his own gang with Bill Dalton called the "Oklahombres." They specialized in bank robberies.

Western History Collections, University of Oklahoma Library

Bob Dalton and Eugenia Moore, three years before Bob was killed in a bank robbery

LAWMEN BANK ROBBERS

Henry Brown and Ben Robertson were both lawmen in Kansas when they robbed the Medicine Valley Bank. Robertson had already fled the law and was living under a new name, Ben Wheeler. They entered the bank on April 30, 1884, along with two other men. During the robbery, Brown killed the bank president and Wheeler killed the cashier. A posse tracked the four outlaws down and jailed them. Wheeler was later lynched and Brown shot down by an angry mob.

Metal bars protected the workers at this Oklahoma bank

On May 20, 1895, the Oklahombres rode into Southwest City, Missouri, and entered the town bank. While they took money from the cashier, a bank official pulled out a gun—and the gang shot him dead. Several townspeople opened fire as the outlaws fled into the street. Doolin spurred his horse, but a bullet hit him in the head as he escaped. He recovered from that wound only to be gunned down a year later.

What may have been the first daylight bank robbery in the U.S. occurred on February 13, 1866, at Liberty, Missouri. Twelve men rode into town and two of them entered the Clay County Savings Bank. The outlaws pulled guns on the cashier, Greenup Bird, and his son. After stuffing $60,000 into a sack, they locked the Birds in the bank vault and left. The riders raced away firing guns and shouting war cries. The outlaws were never caught.

Butch Cassidy had many successes as a bank robber. Seven years before forming his Wild Bunch gang, Cassidy and two others robbed a bank in Telluride, Colorado. They entered the bank and passed a check to the clerk. As the clerk examined the check, they grabbed him and demanded money. They got away with $20,000.

Sometimes even professional robbers panicked during a bank job. In 1896 "Black Jack" Christian and his gang, the "High Fives," held up the International Bank of Nogales in Arizona. As they were leaving, a man started shooting at them. Two of the outlaws panicked, dropped the money, and ran. Christian and the others left the money behind, mounted their horses, and took off.

Roy Daugherty, who called himself "Arkansas Tom Jones," was one bank robber who couldn't go straight. Daugherty rode with the Oklahombre gang until he was captured and sentenced to 50 years in prison. He was released in 1910 and went to Hollywood to act in western movies. But Daugherty returned to bank robbery in 1917. He was jailed two more times, escaped, and was shot down in 1924.

The James-Younger gang held up this Northfield, Minnesota, bank in 1876

Jesse James

Jesse James in 1864, at age 17

Jesse James was one of the most feared outlaws of his time. In the 1860s and 1870s, his James-Younger gang was blamed for nearly every train and bank robbery in Missouri.

Newspapers reported James gang robberies hundreds of miles apart on the same day. Jesse denied the reports in letters to newspaper editors.

Jesse, like many outlaws, got his first taste of violence in the Civil War. His family owned slaves and fought on the side of the South. But Jesse and his brother Frank weren't regular soldiers in uniform. They rode with William Quantrill's raiders in the Kansas-Missouri border wars over slavery.

Jesse claimed he joined the raiders after he and his family were roughed up by Union soldiers. Angry Missourians like Jesse joined Quantrill to fight "Free-Staters" who wanted to end slavery. In 1864 at the age of 17, Jesse rode with rebel leader "Bloody" Bill Anderson. They killed Free-Staters and looted their towns.

After the South lost the war, the rebels in Missouri who had fought for slavery were mistreated by the Union. They lost land, jobs, and property. Jesse decided to get revenge. In February 1866, the James gang robbed their first bank at Liberty, Missouri. They rode out of town shouting war cries and firing guns in the air like Quantrill's raiders had done during the war. One bystander was killed.

Two years later, Jesse and Frank James joined with Cole and Jim Younger to rob a bank at Russelville, Kentucky. They stuffed $12,000 into a grain sack and fled the town. In December 1869, Jesse and Frank entered a bank at Gallatin, Missouri, pretending to be customers. They killed the cashier, wounded a clerk, and took a sack of money. Before they could get away, though, one of their horses ran off. Jesse and Frank jumped onto one horse and raced out of town.

The James brothers were now hunted men, wanted for murder. The Missouri governor offered a reward for their capture.

In 1882, Jesse James had a $10,000 price on his head that many gunmen wanted to collect. Two of them—Charles and Bob Ford—joined Jesse's gang in St. Joseph, Missouri, where Jesse lived under the name of Thomas Howard. On April 3, Jesse was talking with the Fords in his home when he carelessly took off his gun belt and turned to straighten a picture. Bob Ford quickly put a bullet through the back of Jesse's head, then left to collect his reward.

In January 1875, police raided the James farmhouse in Clay County, Missouri, killing Jesse's nine-year-old brother and wounding his mother. Frank and Jesse weren't at home. But news of the raid reached them and fueled their anger.

The James-Younger gang held up the Northfield, Minnesota, bank in 1876. They slashed a cashier's throat and shot a clerk before making their getaway. But a posse quickly caught up to them and wounded Bob Younger. Frank and Jesse wanted to leave him behind, but Bob's brothers refused.

The Jameses escaped on their own and the Youngers were captured.

Jesse kept out of sight for three years, then formed a new gang. They held up trains, banks, and stages until Jesse was killed by a gang member in 1882. Frank James later turned himself in. He was put on trial for murder and found innocent. He lived 30 more years as an honest man and died in old age.

Robbers had to dodge bullets to make a safe getaway

Western History Collections, University of Oklahoma Library

Frank James, Jesse's brother

Billy the Kid

The most famous outlaw of all time was known by many names. He was born William H. Bonney Jr., but took the name Henry McCarty after his father died. He was later called Henry Antrim, Billy Antrim, or Kid Antrim after his mother's second husband. History remembers him as Billy the Kid.

When Billy was 15, his mother died and young Billy took to the streets. He was arrested for stealing clothes, but got away. The Kid fled to Arizona and worked as a cowboy for two years. Then in 1877, he shot and killed a man in an Arizona saloon.

Billy returned to New Mexico and rustled cattle with outlaw Jesse Evans. But he soon left Evans' gang and drifted into Lincoln County. There he worked as a cowboy for ranchers John Tunstall and Alexander McSween.

Billy's bosses were in competition with two other cattlemen named Murphy and Dolan. The Murphy-Dolan gang controlled the local cattle business and sold supplies to ranchers at high prices. Tunstall and McSween tried to cut in on Murphy-Dolan's business.

Billy the Kid

UPI/Bettmann

Western History Collections, University of Oklahoma Library

THE KID AND SHERIFF PAT GARRETT

The Kid and Pat Garrett became friends around 1878 when Garrett was a bartender in Fort Sumner, New Mexico. But their friendship didn't stop Sheriff Garrett from hunting Billy. A few months after the Kid escaped from the Lincoln County jail, Garrett caught up to him at the home of Billy's girlfriend. Garrett hid in a dark room until Billy entered asking, "Who's in there?" Garrett answered with a gunshot to Billy's heart.

Pat Garrett, left, and two other Lincoln County Sheriffs

In the lawless West, disputes like this one were settled with guns. In February 1878, Tunstall was killed by a gang of Murphy-Dolan cowboys. His murder started the Lincoln County War—and the legend of Billy the Kid.

Some stories say that Billy was heartsick at Tunstall's death and vowed to get revenge. But in fact, Billy rode with other cowboy gunmen against Tunstall's killers because McSween paid him to.

In March 1878, Billy and a posse killed two Murphy-Dolan gunmen. A month later, they ambushed Sheriff Brady, who had sided with Murphy-Dolan. Three days later, Billy and others killed Buckshot Roberts, a member of the Murphy-Dolan gang.

Cowboy gunmen on both sides hunted each other for the next three months. Then on July 15, Murphy-Dolan gunmen attacked the Tunstall-McSween gang at McSween's home in Lincoln. This final gunfight of the Lincoln County War lasted four days. On the last day, gunmen set fire to McSween's house. McSween and three of his men were killed. Billy, though, escaped into the night.

With the range war ended, Billy returned to cattle rustling and horse stealing. He was a fugitive, wanted for the murder of Sheriff Brady. In 1879, the Kid turned himself in, hoping for a pardon. But he changed his mind, escaped, and went back to rustling. In 1880, he killed another man in a saloon fight.

Posses led by the new sheriff, Pat Garrett, tried to chase down Billy and his gang. There were several gunfights, but the Kid always got away. Then in December 1880, Garrett's posse surrounded Billy's gang at Stinking Springs. The Kid surrendered.

Billy was tried for murder, found guilty, and sentenced to hang. But the Kid escaped from the Lincoln County jail after killing two guards. A few months later, he was tracked down and killed by Pat Garrett. In his short career as an outlaw, Billy the Kid had killed four men, not the 21 of legend.

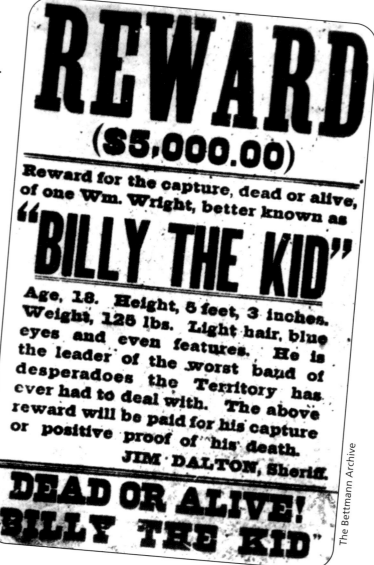

A Billy the Kid "wanted" poster from the 1870s

John Wesley Hardin

Of all western gunmen, John Wesley Hardin was the second most deadly. He killed 11 men in 19 gunfights. Only Jim Miller killed more. Miller, though, was a gunman for hire—he killed for money. Hardin was never a professional killer. He also wasn't a thief. Hardin's only crime was murder. He was a cold-blooded killer.

"Wes" Hardin grew up on the Texas frontier during the Civil War. Like most white Texans of that time, he supported the South and slavery. He could handle a gun and hunt by the age of nine. By the time he was 16, Hardin had turned his gun on four men. First he killed a former slave, then ambushed the three soldiers who came to arrest him. Hardin was a fugitive and outlaw before he was 17 years old.

Family and friends helped young Wes get away. They didn't think it was a crime to kill ex-slaves or the former Union soldiers who policed Texas. Though the Civil War had ended, anger still erupted in feuds and violence against old enemies.

Hardin, though, wasn't out to right the wrongs of the Civil War. He fought his own private war with strangers. Hardin was reckless and quarreled easily. He soon killed a gambler in a dispute over a card game. A month later, he fought with a bully from the circus and shot him in the head. That same month, he killed another man who tried to rob him— shot him between the eyes.

In 1871, the law caught up with Hardin in Marshall, Texas. He was arrested, but escaped after killing a guard. Hardin drifted north, driving cattle up the Chisholm Trail to Abilene. Hardin didn't stay long in Abilene. He soon quarreled with a man and left him lying dead. Hardin drifted back to Texas where he shot two state policemen who were on his trail. One died. Again, Hardin got away.

In July 1872, Hardin was wounded in a gambling argument. He recovered and joined his cousins in the Sutton-Taylor feud. Hardin killed a sheriff who was an enemy of the Taylors, and the sheriff's deputy as well. But the law was closing in.

John Wesley Hardin

Texas Rangers taking a chow break at Fort McKavett

Hardin celebrated his twenty-first birthday at the horse races in Comanche, Texas, with his brother Joe and friends. In a Comanche saloon, Deputy Sheriff Webb approached Hardin and they argued. Webb drew his pistol, but was gunned down by Hardin and his friends. An angry mob lynched Hardin's brother and friends, but Wes escaped. There was now a $4,000 reward for Hardin—dead or alive.

Hardin left Texas for Florida with his wife and child and tried to reform. He changed his name and started several businesses. But the Texas Rangers tracked him down and captured him on a train. Hardin served 17 years in Texas state prison, where he spent his time studying law. After his release in 1894, he became a lawyer—but not for long. On August 19, 1895, Hardin was shot in the back of the head while gambling in an El Paso saloon.

Hardin studied in prison to become a lawyer

HARDIN MEETS HICKOK

Legend says Wes Hardin had a small run-in with Abilene town marshal Wild Bill Hickok in 1871. Supposedly, Hickok asked Hardin to hand over his guns, since Abilene had a law against carrying firearms. Hardin held out his pistols with the handles facing Hickok, then spun them around, barrels pointing at the lawman. This trick was called the "road agent's spin." The story is probably untrue. Only Hardin himself remembered the incident.

Joaquin Murrieta

The legend of Joaquin Murrieta, like all outlaw legends, is part fiction and part fact. Some say he never existed or that the crimes of different men were blamed on one. Others insist there truly was one outlaw named Joaquin Murrieta who led a gang of bandits during the California Gold Rush.

California was settled by Spanish ranchers from Mexico a hundred years before the gold rush. In fact, California belonged to Mexico until 1848, when the U.S. won the Mexican War. Gold was discovered the same year and gold seekers rushed in.

Without lawmen and courts, theft and violence ruled in the gold fields of California's Calaveras County. Most of the victims were Mexican, Chilean, and Chinese miners. White miners, fearing competition, attacked non-whites and passed laws against them. Spanish-speaking *Californios* were driven from their homes or killed. One of these *Californios* was Joaquin Murrieta.

Gambling and drinking often led to violence in California's gold fields

THE BALLAD OF GREGORIO CORTEZ

Gregorio Cortez was a peaceful Mexican American rancher in Texas when his trouble started. In June 1901, a sheriff and deputy wrongly accused Cortez of horse theft and shot his brother. Cortez returned the fire and killed the sheriff. Fearing a lynch mob, he fled. Cortez traveled more than 500 miles in ten days to avoid capture. He was finally caught and served 12 years in prison. Mexicans on the Texas border tell his story in folk songs called *corridos*.

Cortez's story became the subject of Mexican folk songs

Legend says that Joaquin had been a gold prospector until white miners beat him up and forced him out. Angry and bitter, Joaquin formed a band of outlaws to steal gold from white men. He wasn't the only one.

During the 1850s, many outlaw gangs raided the gold fields. Some, like Joaquin's, were formed by Mexican Americans. Other gangs were started by white men. These bandits stole horses, robbed stagecoaches, and killed for gold. It was said that Joaquin stole only from whites, but actually most of his victims were Chinese.

In November 1852, someone stole a hundred horses and killed a white man in San Gabriel. Joaquin

Non-white miners were often robbed and attacked

Murrieta and other Mexican Americans were accused of the crimes. Several of the *Californios* were lynched by vigilantes, but Murrieta got away. Soon other crimes in gold country were blamed on Murrieta's gang.

Hundreds of vigilantes rode after Joaquin. In February 1853, a gang of Mexican Americans killed six Chinese men at the Big Bar mining camp and stole $6,000 in gold. Nine more Chinese and one white American were robbed and killed the following week. Murrieta was blamed.

California's governor offered a $1,000 reward for Joaquin's capture. But no one really knew what he looked like. Some thought that "Three-Fingered Jack" Garcia was part of Joaquin's gang. But no one knew for sure.

The Murrieta gang was difficult to track. They rode fast horses and they knew the old Spanish trails.

In May, a posse of California Rangers was formed to capture or kill Joaquin. They tracked his gang for two months and caught up to him in the San Joaquin Valley. The Rangers attacked and killed Joaquin, "Three-Fingered Jack" Garcia, and two other gang members. They cut off Joaquin's head and Garcia's hand as proof.

Joaquin's head was preserved in alcohol and put on display until it was lost in the San Francisco earthquake. But many doubted that the head was really Joaquin's. Some legends say he escaped to Mexico.

Belle Starr

Belle Starr was the "Bandit Queen" of Oklahoma Territory in the days before it was a state. In Belle's time Oklahoma was Indian Territory and not open to white settlers. But white outlaws and bandits escaped to hideouts in Indian country to avoid arrest. Belle Starr helped many of them and also married a few.

Belle was born in Missouri and moved with her family to Texas when she was 16. Her brother Ed fought with Quantrill's raiders in the Kansas-Missouri border wars. Quantrill and other Missourians were pro-slavery and fought for the South. When Ed was killed by soldiers, Belle vowed to get revenge.

Wanted poster for Sam and Belle Starr, formerly Belle Shirley

Belle Starr, armed with two pistols

In Texas, Belle married a Quantrill raider named Jim Reed. In 1869, she gave birth to a daughter, who was sent to live with Reed's mother. Around this time, Reed killed a man who had killed his brother. Belle and Reed fled into Indian Territory to escape Texas state police. They were on the run for two years and lived in California and Mexico before returning to Texas.

Back in Texas, Belle opened a gambling saloon while Reed hid out from police. Belle became friendly with the Younger brothers and other outlaws during this time. But soon Reed was arrested for robbery and sent to jail. Belle vowed to kill the deputy who arrested him. She helped Reed escape by switching clothes during a visit. Reed walked out of jail disguised as Belle. Some time later, the deputy was killed. His murderer was never found.

In 1873, Reed, Belle, and two other men tortured and robbed an Indian chief in Indian Territory. They took $30,000 that was hidden under the chief's cabin. A year later, Reed robbed a stage in Texas and a $4,000 reward was offered for his capture. He was shot dead by a friend who collected the reward.

HENRY STARR, CHEROKEE OUTLAW

Henry Starr was one of the last and most daring of western bank robbers. He was part Cherokee Indian and related to bandit Belle Starr by marriage. In 1891, he robbed the Missouri Pacific Railroad and, five months later, killed the lawman who came to arrest him. Starr was later caught and served 19 years in federal prison. After his release in 1915, Starr and six others robbed two Oklahoma banks on the same morning. He was killed in 1921 during another bank holdup.

Henry Starr in 1919

Belle went on with her outlaw life. She ran a horse stable near Dallas and hid stolen horses for the James-Younger gang. She was arrested for horse theft in 1878, but escaped by charming a deputy into letting her go. Two years later, Belle married a Cherokee Indian named Sam Starr. They settled on Indian land along the Canadian River and called their home Younger's Bend.

Belle's home became a hideout and social spot for outlaws. Jesse James and other members of the James gang visited there. But Indian Territory was under the watchful eye of federal judge Isaac Parker. In 1882, Parker had Belle and Sam arrested for horse theft. They served nine months in federal prison, then returned to Younger's Bend.

Belle and Sam continued their horse thieving and were arrested again. Belle was found innocent, but Sam was charged with other crimes. In 1887, Sam was shot dead at a dance. Belle soon took up with Sam's cousin, outlaw Henry Starr. In 1889, Belle was ambushed and killed while riding near her home. Her murderer was believed to be another horse thief.

Jim Reed escaped from jail disguised as Belle

The Daltons

The Dalton brothers—Bob, Grat, and Emmett—had short but active outlaw careers. They robbed trains in and around Oklahoma for just two years before turning to bank robbery. They had no luck with banks, however. The Dalton gang bit the dust while trying to rob two Kansas banks on the same day.

The Daltons, like many other outlaws, began their gunfighting careers as lawmen. Their older brother Frank Dalton had been a deputy U.S. marshal. After he was killed by outlaws in Indian Territory, Bob, Grat, and Emmett tried to live up to Frank's good name. They became deputy U.S. marshals—but their law careers didn't last long.

Grat and Emmett were accused of cattle rustling and forced to quit their jobs. Meanwhile, Bob was fired for taking bribes. Bob and Emmett then headed for New Mexico, while Grat joined another brother, Bill, in California.

The Condon Bank, one of the two banks the Daltons tried to rob in Coffeyville, Kansas

Western History Collections, University of Oklahoma Library

Bob and Emmett formed an outlaw gang and robbed a gamblers' hangout near Silver City, New Mexico, in 1890. It was the Dalton brothers' first robbery. Bob escaped to California and Emmett fled into Oklahoma Territory.

In 1891, Bob joined Grat and two others for a train robbery in California. The outlaws tore open the express car with axes and shot down the fireman as he ran for help. But they couldn't open the safe. The Daltons escaped empty-handed. Grat was later caught and sent to jail, but he escaped on the way.

Bob fled California and met up with Emmett back in Oklahoma. In May 1891, Bob, Emmett, and two others robbed a train near Perry, Oklahoma. They held the train crew at gunpoint and took the express sack. But the outlaws had been tricked. The sack was stuffed with telegrams and mail.

Western History Collections, University of Oklahoma Library

Mrs. Louis Dalton, mother of the Dalton brothers

The Dalton gang rode into Coffeyville wearing fake beards and mustaches

Grat rejoined his brothers after escaping California lawmen. They hid out in Oklahoma hill country where they formed a gang of train robbers. The gang included Bill Doolin, Dick Broadwell, Bill Powers, and others. During the next year, the Dalton gang robbed four trains in Oklahoma Territory. Their last train robbery took place in July 1892. They were ambushed by four lawmen, but escaped into the Dog Creek Hills after wounding all four. They soon began planning their next job. It was to be their biggest, but it turned out to be their last.

The Dalton gang rode into Coffeyville, Kansas, on October 5, 1892, disguised in fake beards and mustaches. They planned to rob two town banks. But news of their plan had leaked out. Bob and Emmett entered one bank, while Grat, Powers, and Broadwell entered the other. Townspeople waited in hiding outside with Winchester rifles.

Four Dalton gang members killed during the Coffeyville robbery

The outlaws filled their money sacks and headed for the bank doors. As they stepped into the street, the shooting started. When the smoke cleared, Bob and Grat were dead. So were Broadwell, Powers, and three townspeople. Emmett was badly wounded, but survived. The Dalton gang had met a bloody end.

AFTER COFFEYVILLE

After the Coffeyville holdup, Emmett Dalton was sentenced to life in prison. In 1907, though, he was pardoned and released. After prison, Emmett married and went into business, then moved to Hollywood to write and act in movies. Meanwhile, Bill Dalton turned to a life of crime. Bill had never been part of the Dalton gang. But after Bob and Grat Dalton were killed and Emmett jailed for life, Bill joined the Oklahombres gang to get even. He was killed by a posse in 1895.

Butch Cassidy and the Wild Bunch

Butch Cassidy was one of the last frontier outlaws and probably the best outlaw gang leader. By the time he formed his Wild Bunch gang in 1896, the western frontier was closed. Law and order had caught up to the Wild West. Rustlers, horse thieves, and stage, train, and bank robbers would soon be history. Cassidy's Wild Bunch was the last and biggest gang ever to ride the Outlaw Trail.

Cassidy's real name was Robert LeRoy Parker. He was born on a Utah ranch in 1867, the year of the first cattle drives to Abilene. He learned to ride, shoot, and herd cattle from an outlaw cowboy named Mike Cassidy. As a teenager, Parker took the name George Cassidy in honor of his outlaw hero.

In November 1887, George Cassidy joined the McCarty gang for his first train robbery. But the outlaws left empty-handed after an express agent refused to open the safe. In 1889, Cassidy and the McCartys held up two Colorado banks and got away with $30,000.

Butch Cassidy

Cassidy then headed for Wyoming, where he worked as a cowboy and rustled cattle. In 1892, he took a job in a Rock Springs, Wyoming, butcher shop, and townspeople began calling him "Butch." He quit the job, but kept the name when he went back to rustling and horse stealing. In 1894, Butch Cassidy was arrested and sent to state prison for two years. It was the first and last time the law caught up with him.

Outlaw women were members of the Hole in the Wall gang

Western History Collections, University of Oklahoma Library

ESCAPE TO SOUTH AMERICA

Though Butch Cassidy never killed a man, he was one of the most hunted outlaws of his day. To avoid capture, Cassidy and his partners, the Sundance Kid and Etta Place, fled to Argentina in 1902. They raised cattle and sheep, then began holding up banks in Bolivia. In 1908, Butch and Sundance were ambushed by the Bolivian army. Some say they were both killed, while others insist they escaped to the United States, changed their names, and lived to old age.

Butch was released in 1896 and began riding the Outlaw Trail, a network of secret trails in remote country that ran from northern Wyoming down to Mexico. Many outlaw cowboys rode these trails beginning in the 1880s, when fences, blizzards, and changing times were putting cowboys out of work.

Cassidy began organizing these outlaws. He and his gang used Wyoming's Hole-in-the-Wall country as a hideout. At saloons in Rock Springs, people began calling Butch's gang the "Wild Bunch."

In 1897, Cassidy and outlaw Elza Lay stole $8,000 in payroll money from the Castle Gate mining camp in Utah. News of the daring holdup spread up and down the Outlaw Trail. More and more outlaws joined Butch's gang, including the "Sundance Kid," whose real name was Harry Longabaugh.

Butch Cassidy (seated right) and the Wild Bunch

When they weren't raiding cattle and horses, the outlaws threw wild parties at their hideouts. Outlaw women such as Laura Bullion and Etta Place kept company with Butch and his gang.

Around 1898, Cassidy formed his "Train Robber's Syndicate" to hold up gold shipments on Union Pacific trains. In June 1899, the Wild Bunch used a little too much dynamite to open an express car safe at Wilcox, Wyoming. The whole car was blown apart and money fell like rain.

Other train and bank robberies followed, but just as outlaws had become more organized, so had lawmen. The railroads hired Pinkerton police and "super posses" to track the Wild Bunch. With the law closing in, Butch fled to South America in 1902.

Laura Bullion

Bat Masterson

Bat Masterson was never the gunfighter he claimed to be. During his career as a lawman, Masterson was in three gunfights and killed one man. He lived longer than most gunmen, though, and spent his last twenty years as a newspaper reporter in New York. As a writer, Masterson helped create his own gunfighter legend.

Around 1872, Bat and his brothers Ed and Jim Masterson left the family farm near Wichita, Kansas, and headed west to Dodge City. They worked for the railroad as buffalo sharpshooters for several years.

After that, Masterson worked as a scout for the U.S. Army. He soon quit and began drifting around Texas. He gambled, prowled the saloons, and got into his first gunfight. On January 23, 1876, Bat shot and killed U.S. Army Sergeant King in a saloon fight over a woman. King is the only man known to have been killed by Masterson.

Bat Masterson

By 1877, the Masterson brothers were back in Dodge City, where Bat owned a saloon. Dodge was a booming cowtown filled with rowdy cowboys just off the trails. Ed Masterson soon became town deputy marshal and Bat was made county sheriff.

The Mastersons' reputation as sharpshooters helped them keep the peace in Dodge. Few cowboys or local gamblers wanted to tangle with them. But there were exceptions. In April 1878, Ed was killed while trying to disarm a drunken cowboy. Bat and the townspeople took Ed's death hard. Jim Masterson reacted by becoming a lawman.

The Masterson brothers worked as buffalo sharpshooters for the railroad

Newspapers in 1882 claimed that Bat Masterson had killed 22 men. Though Masterson knew the stories were lies, he never corrected them. Like most gunfighters, he liked the publicity. In time, Masterson began writing his own magazine articles about frontier gunfights. He even bought an old Colt pistol, cut 22 notches in the handle to represent the men he had supposedly killed, and sold it to a collector. In the end, Masterson's pen was more powerful than his six-gun.

Bat made Jim a deputy sheriff. Jim also served on the Dodge City police force with Wyatt Earp. In July 1878, Jim and Wyatt opened fire on a gang of cowboys who were out on a shooting spree. As the gang rode off, one wounded outlaw fell from his horse.

In January 1879, Sheriff Bat Masterson was made deputy U.S. marshal. These two jobs, however, didn't stop Bat from taking a third. In March, he was hired as a gunman for the Santa Fe Railroad. It was a mistake. Citizens didn't believe that Masterson took his law duties seriously. In the next election for sheriff, Bat Masterson was defeated.

Bat left Dodge City to become a professional gambler in Colorado. In 1881, he drifted into Tombstone, Arizona. But in April, Bat received word that his brother Jim needed help back in Dodge. Jim had quarreled with partners in a saloon business and the men were gunning for him. Bat hopped the next train to Dodge City.

Moments after Bat arrived in Dodge, a gunfight erupted on the main street. Bat and his friends fought Jim's enemies in the Battle of the Plaza. No one was actually killed, but the gunfight sparked stories about the "killer gunman" Bat Masterson.

The Bettmann Archive

Bat Masterson (standing, right) and Wyatt Earp (seated, second from left) were members of the Dodge City Peace Commission

Newspapers said he'd killed seven men in revenge for his brother Ed, and shot two more defending Jim. Masterson never denied the rumors. He returned to gambling and later became a sports writer. He died in 1921 while writing a news story.

Wild Bill Hickok

SHERIFF

Wild Bill Hickok was a sharpshooting lawman and a legend in his own time. Magazine stories and picture books called him the "Prince of the Pistoleers." But the facts of Hickok's life and his talent as a gunman are amazing even without the tall tales.

James Butler Hickok got his first taste of action while helping his father on the Underground Railroad. The Underground Railroad was a secret network of people who helped slaves escape to the northern states, where they could be free.

Around 1861, Hickok took a job with the Overland Stage Company in Rock Creek, Nebraska. While in Rock Creek, Hickok shot and killed a rancher named Dave McCanles in a dispute over a woman. Although McCanles was unarmed at the time, the local judge let Hickok go.

Hickok headed for the Missouri border and worked as a scout and spy for the Union Army. After the Civil War, he became a gambler in Springfield, Missouri, where he quarreled with Dave Tutt over a woman and a card game. The next day, he shot and killed Tutt in the public square after Tutt fired first. A magazine writer stretched the facts of the case, turning "Wild Bill" Hickok into a western hero.

Hickok returned to Kansas, where his gun skills were in demand. He worked as a deputy U.S. marshal, then as an army scout for Gen. George Custer's Seventh Cavalry. In 1868, he captured 11 army deserters. That same year, he rescued 34 cowboys who were trapped by Cheyenne Indians in Colorado Territory.

Hickok became city marshal of Abilene in 1871. He split his time between gambling and enforcing the law. Wild Bill was feared and respected as a sharpshooter, but also disliked by Abilene's rowdy Texas cowboys and gamblers. Two of these gamblers, Phil Coe and Ben Thompson, tried to hire the Texas outlaw Wes Hardin to kill Hickok. But Hardin knew better than to mess with Wild Bill. Hickok was always on guard to keep from being shot in the back.

Western History Collections, University of Oklahoma Library

Wild Bill Hickok

The "dead man's hand"

In October, Phil Coe and a crowd of Texas cowboys went on a drunken spree through Abilene. Hickok caught up to them after Coe fired a shot in front of the Alamo saloon. Wild Bill drew his pistol, but Coe's was already out. Coe fired and missed, then Hickok gunned him down. But in the confusion Hickok also killed his own deputy. Wild Bill was finished in Abilene.

Hickok worked the next few years in Buffalo Bill's Wild West Show. Around 1876, he showed up in the Dakota mining town of Deadwood. Hickok spent his time playing poker, but didn't watch his back as he had done in Abilene. In August, Wild Bill was shot in the back of the head by a man named McCall. Hickok had just been dealt his poker hand—a queen, two aces, and two eights—which came to be called the "dead man's hand."

HICKOK THE SHARPSHOOTER

Wyatt Earp claimed he saw Wild Bill fire ten shots through the letter "O" of a sign from 100 yards away. In fact, Earp never met Hickok. Outlaw legends always stretched the truth. In target shooting contests with marksmen Frank North and John Talbot, Hickok came in third. In actual gunfights, though, Hickok was the deadly best. No other gunman had Wild Bill's ability to aim straight while being shot at. And though Wild Bill could shoot with either hand, he never used his left in a gunfight.

It was said that Wild Bill could fire a bullet through an "O"

Bass Reeves

Bass Reeves, U.S. marshal

After the Civil War, freed African American slaves moved west for a better life. Some drifted into Indian Territory in what is now Oklahoma. The U.S. government had set aside this territory for Native American tribes. Whites couldn't settle there. But some blacks, like Bass Reeves, were welcomed by the Indians.

Reeves had been born into slavery and was 25 when he gained his freedom. He worked his way west to Indian Territory, where he became a deputy U.S. marshal in 1875.

All lawmen in Indian Territory worked for the U.S. government—state and local lawmen had no authority there. Many outlaws escaped to Indian country to avoid arrest. But Bass Reeves and the U.S. marshals were waiting for them.

Reeves was powerfully built and a dead-eye gunman. He spoke Creek and other Indian languages and was respected by the tribes. Indians knew that blacks were mistreated by whites, just as Indians were. Reeves used his skills and his contacts among Native Americans to track cattle rustlers and horse thieves in Indian Territory.

Between 1875 and 1907, Reeves worked as a deputy for seven different U.S. marshals. He claimed to have killed 14 outlaws in the line of duty without ever being injured. He was shot at many times, though, and had some close calls. Outlaw bullets nicked his clothes and grazed his horse, but never hit him.

AFRICAN-INDIAN LAWMEN

Escaped slaves lived among the Seminole Indians in Florida until the 1840s. After their defeat in the Seminole Wars, these "black Indians" were forced to move west to Indian Territory. In 1870, the U.S. Army formed a special troop of black Seminoles to fight outlaws and Comanches in Texas. They rode, scouted, and fought like Indian warriors in 26 battles along the Texas border. In nine years of fighting, not one scout was killed or wounded.

Indians respected Bass Reeves

Indians who knew Reeves believed he had strong "medicine," or inner power. Either they were right or Reeves was just plain lucky. Reeves never learned to read or write, but he could read the land and understood nature's signals. These skills helped him track outlaws along the trails through Indian country. Reeves claimed he always brought in the men he went after—except once. Reeves tried to chase down an outlaw named "Hellubee Sammy" in Okfuskee County, but the outlaw had a faster horse and got away. In another chase, Reeves somehow rounded up more than a dozen horse thieves and hauled them to jail.

Bass Reeves wasn't the only African American lawman in Indian Territory, but he was probably the best. He was also one of the most creative lawmen anywhere on the frontier. He often wore disguises to get close to the men he was tracking.

Disguised as a beggar, Reeves once entered the home of two wanted men. He ate dinner with them and shared a few laughs before bedding down on their floor. In the middle of the night, Reeves handcuffed the outlaws while they slept. The next day, he marched his prisoners to jail and collected his reward.

Bass Reeves is one of many little-known black lawmen of the old West. He was almost 70 when he retired from the U.S. marshal's office in Oklahoma. Even then, law enforcement was still in his blood. He worked as a policeman in Muskogee County until 1909 and died soon after he quit.

Reeves captured some outlaws while they slept

"Hangin' Judge" Isaac Parker

Isaac Parker was one of the busiest and bravest of frontier judges. During his 21 years as a federal judge, Parker convicted 9,000 outlaws out of the 13,500 brought to his court. Exactly 88 of them died by hanging. Newspapers called Parker the "Hangin' Judge." His courtroom was nicknamed "Hell on the Border." Parker was tough on crime, but he was also honest and fair.

Parker's court was in Fort Smith, Arkansas, but he also had authority over Indian Territory. Thieves and murderers escaped state and local lawmen by crossing onto Indian lands. Only U.S. marshals and deputies working for Judge Parker could arrest them in Indian Territory.

Parker was serious about catching outlaws and bringing them to trial. He started by appointing 200 deputy U.S. marshals to bring them in. Sixty-five deputies died trying. But after just 50 days on the job, Parker had held 91 trials and sentenced eight men to be hanged. On September 3, 1875, six of those men were taken to the gallows.

Judge Isaac Parker

Hanging was a popular form of entertainment on the western frontier. Some 5,000 men, women, and children crowded the courtyard at Fort Smith to watch Judge Parker's sentence carried out. A noose was placed around each prisoner's neck and the trap door opened. It was the first of many such hangings.

Parker's prisoners lived in dark, crowded, basement cells until a new jailhouse was built in 1877. The new jail was supposed to hold 144 prisoners, two to a cell, but more were often packed in.

Parker put in long hours and tried each case carefully. He took time to be certain that those on trial understood the lawyers. Innocence or guilt was decided by a jury. Parker made certain that jurors also understood everything that was said in court. Every trial was legal and fair.

Judge Parker sent many outlaws to the gallows

The Big Bend country of Texas was a mountain hiding place for outlaws west of the Pecos River. Gangs of thieves proved there was "no law west of the Pecos"—until Roy Bean arrived, that is. Bean was justice of the peace in Langtry, Texas, and a citizen judge in local "people's courts." Though he was not a legal judge, Bean helped bring law and order to a wild country. He never hanged an outlaw. Instead, he took their money and ran them out of the territory.

Western History Collections, University of Oklahoma Library

Ten deputy U.S. marshals appointed by Judge Parker

Seven months after the first hanging, five more outlaws were hanged on the gallows outside Judge Parker's window. This time 6,000 people crowded the courtyard to watch the hangman carry out Parker's sentence.

In 1882, one of Parker's marshals arrested the outlaw Belle Starr and her husband Sam Starr for horse stealing. A jury found them guilty and Judge Parker sentenced them to a year in the Detroit House of Correction in Michigan.

Four years later, an outlaw friend of Belle's named "Blue Duck" was found guilty of murder in Parker's court. He was sentenced to hang, but Belle hired a lawyer to stop the hanging. His sentence was changed to life in prison after his lawyer appealed to the president of the United States.

In 1895, Parker sentenced the outlaw "Cherokee Bill" to hang for several murders, including one of a prison guard at Parker's jail. A year later, Parker died after 21 years as the "Hangin' Judge." He'd brought law and order to a wild frontier.

Judge Parker sentenced Cherokee Bill to hang

Western History Collections, University of Oklahoma Library

Wyatt Earp

The Earp brothers and Doc Holliday took part in the most famous gunfight in western history at the OK Corral in Tombstone, Arizona. Wyatt Earp's career as a lawman and gunfighter began 12 years earlier. He was a town policeman in Missouri, but was run out of town with his brothers after causing a street fight. He was later arrested in Indian Territory for horse stealing.

Earp became a gambler and buffalo hunter, then deputy marshal of Wichita. He wound up in Dodge City as a lawman, then drifted into Texas on the trail of cattle thieves. There he became friends with a dentist and gambler named Doc Holliday.

Late in 1879, Wyatt, James, and Virgil Earp moved to Tombstone and were joined there by their brothers Morgan and Warren, and Doc Holliday. Tombstone was a tough town on the mining frontier. Wyatt became deputy sheriff, but lost the job to a man named Behan. Behan later became sheriff. The Earps and Holliday took to gambling and Wyatt was hired as a saloon guard.

In March 1881, a stagecoach was held up near Tombstone and the driver killed. Sheriff Behan blamed Doc Holliday and arrested him. Wyatt in turn accused Behan and his cowboy friends the Clanton and McLaury brothers. When Virgil Earp became marshal in June, he had Holliday released. But a feud was starting. Virgil quickly made his brothers and Holliday deputy marshals.

Wyatt Earp

The OK Corral in Tombstone, Arizona

On October 25, Ike Clanton and Tom McLaury began threatening the Earps and Holliday. Holliday cursed Clanton, and Virgil Earp clubbed Clanton with a gun. The next morning, Wyatt clubbed Tom McLaury with his pistol. That afternoon, he picked a fight with Frank McLaury. Frank backed off and headed for the OK Corral.

At the corral, Frank met up with his brother Tom, Ike and Billy Clanton, and another cowboy named Bill Claiborne. People disagree about what exactly happened next. Some say the cowboys kept threatening the lawmen; others say they simply prepared to leave town.

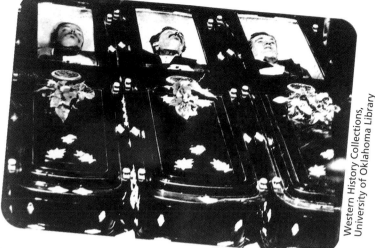

Tom and Frank McLaury and Billy Clanton, killed at the OK Corral

The Earps and Doc Holliday gathered and walked toward the corral. Sheriff Behan tried to head off trouble by asking the Clantons and McLaurys to give up their weapons. Frank refused. Ike and Tom claimed to be unarmed. Behan then warned Virgil Earp not to start a gunfight. Virgil claimed he just wanted to disarm the cowboys.

As they approached the corral, the Earps and Holliday spread out. Virgil called for the cowboys to surrender—then the shooting started. Morgan Earp fired the first shot. It hit teenage Billy Clanton, who later died. Wyatt fired at Frank, wounding him badly, but Frank kept shooting, hitting Morgan. Morgan returned the fire, killing Frank.

Ike Clanton, who was unarmed, ran toward Wyatt begging him to stop shooting. Wyatt pushed him away and Ike, along with Bill Claiborne, fled the scene. Holliday killed Tom McLaury with a round of buckshot and the gunfight ended. The shootout at the OK Corral had lasted thirty seconds and left three men dead. Wyatt Earp wasn't even scratched. Though some blamed the Earps for the fight and called them murderers, Wyatt's fame as a lawman grew.

DOC HOLLIDAY

Wyatt Earp's friend Doc Holliday had an advantage over other gunmen. Around the time he finished dentistry school, Holliday became ill and was told he didn't have long to live. Since Doc knew he'd die soon, he feared no man's gun. He quit dentistry and turned to drinking and gambling. He was in eight gunfights and killed at least two men. He died at 35 of lung disease.

Doc Holliday

Violence and Guns in America Today

Violence in America did not end with the close of the western frontier. The culture of violence and guns that exploded in the Wild West is still with us. Colt six-guns, though, have been replaced by more modern and accurate pistols.

Today, automatic rifles and semiautomatic handguns are easy to buy and easier to use than Old West Winchesters and "Peacemakers." But guns still don't make peace—except by death.

In 1990, there were more than 10,000 deaths caused by handguns in the United States. In the same year, there were only 87 handgun deaths in Japan and just 22 in Great Britain. It's no wonder that many Americans want laws to control the sale of handguns.

On American streets, automatic assault rifles are in the hands of drug dealers and gangs. Bullets are used to commit crimes and to settle arguments. Innocent victims are often killed in drive-by shootings. Some students even carry weapons to school. The culture of gun violence has gotten worse, not better, since the days of the Wild West.

The National Rifle Association insists that all adult Americans without criminal records have a constitutional right to own firearms. Others disagree. In national polls, half of American citizens are against owning handguns. Some 49 percent would vote for a ban on all handguns except those used by law officers.

In 1993, President Bill Clinton signed a gun control law limiting the sale of handguns. This law requires a five-day waiting period on handgun purchases. Supporters of gun control hope this law will keep guns out of the hands of criminals. Handguns may someday be completely outlawed in the United States. Meanwhile, gun violence continues as law officers and concerned citizens try to stop it.

President Clinton signed a gun control law in 1993

INDEX

EXTREMELY WEIRD SERIES

All of the titles are written by Sarah Lovett, 8½" x 11", 48 pages, $9.95 paperbacks, with color photographs and illustrations

Extremely Weird Bats
Extremely Weird Birds
Extremely Weird Endangered Species
Extremely Weird Fishes
Extremely Weird Frogs
Extremely Weird Insects
Extremely Weird Mammals
Extremely Weird Micro Monsters
Extremely Weird Primates
Extremely Weird Reptiles
Extremely Weird Sea Creatures
Extremely Weird Snakes
Extremely Weird Spiders

X-RAY VISION SERIES

Each title in the series is 8½" x 11", 48 pages, $9.95 paperback, with color photographs and illustrations, and written by Ron Schultz.

Looking Inside the Brain
Looking Inside Cartoon Animation
Looking Inside Caves and Caverns
Looking Inside Sports Aerodynamics
Looking Inside Sunken Treasure
Looking Inside Telescopes and the Night Sky

THE KIDDING AROUND TRAVEL GUIDES

All of the titles listed below are 64 pages and $9.95 paperbacks, except for *Kidding Around the National Parks* and *Kidding Around Spain*, which are 108 pages and $12.95 paperbacks.

Kidding Around Atlanta
Kidding Around Boston, 2nd ed.
Kidding Around Chicago, 2nd ed.
Kidding Around the Hawaiian Islands
Kidding Around London
Kidding Around Los Angeles
Kidding Around the National Parks of the Southwest
Kidding Around New York City, 2nd ed.
Kidding Around Paris
Kidding Around Philadelphia
Kidding Around San Diego
Kidding Around San Francisco
Kidding Around Santa Fe
Kidding Around Seattle
Kidding Around Spain
Kidding Around Washington, D.C., 2nd ed.

MASTERS OF MOTION SERIES

Each title in the series is 10¼" x 9", 48 pages, $9.95 paperback, with color photographs and illustrations.

How to Drive an Indy Race Car
  David Rubel
How to Fly a 747
  Tim Paulson
How to Fly the Space Shuttle
  Russell Shorto

THE KIDS EXPLORE SERIES

Each title is written by kids for kids by the Westridge Young Writers Workshop, 7" x 9", and $9.95 paperback, with photographs and illustrations by the kids.

Kids Explore America's Hispanic Heritage 112 pages
Kids Explore America's African American Heritage 128 pages
Kids Explore the Gifts of Children with Special Needs 128 pages
Kids Explore America's Japanese American Heritage 144 pages

ENVIRONMENTAL TITLES

Habitats: *Where the Wild Things Live*
Randi Hacker and Jackie Kaufman
8½" x 11", 48 pages, color illustrations, $9.95 paper

The Indian Way: *Learning to Communicate with Mother Earth*
Gary McLain
7" x 9", 114 pages, two-color illustrations, $9.95 paper

Rads, Ergs, and Cheeseburgers: *The Kids' Guide to Energy and the Environment*
Bill Yanda
7" x 9", 108 pages, two-color illustrations, $13.95 paper

The Kids' Environment Book: *What's Awry and Why*
Anne Pedersen
7" x 9", 192 pages, two-color illustrations, $13.95 paper

BIZARRE & BEAUTIFUL SERIES

A spirited and fun investigation of the mysteries of the five senses in the animal kingdom.

Each title in the series is 8½" x 11", $14.95 hardcover, with color photographs and illustrations throughout.

Bizarre & Beautiful Ears
Bizarre & Beautiful Eyes
Bizarre & Beautiful Feelers
Bizarre & Beautiful Noses
Bizarre & Beautiful Tongues

RAINBOW WARRIOR SERIES

W hat is a Rainbow Warrior Artist? It is a person who strives to live in harmony with the Earth and all living creatures, and who tries to better the world while living his or her life in a creative way.

Each title is written by Reavis Moore with a foreword by LeVar Burton, and is 8½" x 11", 48 pages, $14.95 hardcover, with color photographs and illustrations.

Native Artists of Africa
Native Artists of North America
Native Artists of Europe (available 9/94)

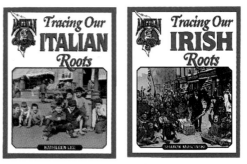

ROUGH AND READY SERIES

L earn about the men and women who settled the American West. Explore the myths and legends about these courageous individuals and learn about the environmental, cultural, and economic legacies they left to us.

Each title in the series is written by A. S. Gintzler and is 48 pages, 8½" x 11", $12.95 hardcover, with two-color illustrations and duotone archival photographs.

Available 7/94:

Rough and Ready Cowboys
Rough and Ready Homesteaders
Rough and Ready Prospectors

Rough and Ready Loggers
Rough and Ready
  Outlaws & Lawmen
Rough and Ready Railroaders

AMERICAN ORIGINS SERIES

M any of us are the third and fourth generation of our families to live in America. Learn what our great-great-grandparents experienced when they arrived here and how much of our lives are still intertwined with theirs.

Each title is 48 pages, 8½" x 11", $12.95 hardcover, with two-color illustrations and duotone archival photographs.

Available 6/94:

Tracing Our German Roots
Tracing Our Irish Roots
Tracing Our Italian Roots
Tracing Our Jewish Roots

Tracing Our Chinese Roots
Tracing Our Japanese Roots
Tracing Our Polish Roots

ORDERING INFORMATION
Please check your local bookstore for our books, or call 1-800-888-7504 to order direct from us. All orders are shipped via UPS; see chart below to calculate your shipping charge for U.S. destinations. **No P.O. Boxes please; we must have a street address to ensure delivery.** If the book you request is not available, we will hold your check until we can ship it. Foreign orders will be shipped surface rate unless otherwise requested; please enclose $3.00 for the first item and $1.00 for each additional item.

METHOD OF PAYMENT
Check, money order, American Express, MasterCard, or VISA. We cannot be responsible for cash sent through the mail. For credit card orders, include your card number, expiration date, and your signature, or call 1-800-888-7504. American Express card orders can be shipped only to billing address of card holder. Sorry, no C.O.D.'s. Residents of sunny New Mexico, add 6.25% tax to total.

Address all orders and inquiries to: John Muir Publications
P.O. Box 613
Santa Fe, NM 87504

(505) 982-4078
(800) 888-7504

For U.S. Orders Totaling	Add
Up to $15.00	$4.25
$15.01 to $45.00	$5.25
$45.01 to $75.00	$6.25
$75.01 or more	$7.25

DATE DUE

JAN 25 2001			

GAYLORD

PRINTED IN U.S.A.